DK Life Stories
Martin Luther King Jr

DK Life Stories
Martin Luther King Jr

by Laurie Calkhoven

Illustrated by Charlotte Ager

Editor Allison Singer
Senior Designer Joanne Clark

Project Editor Roohi Sehgal
Editor Radhika Haswani
Additional Editorial Kritika Gupta
Art Editor Kanika Kalra
Project Art Editor Yamini Panwar
Jacket Coordinator Francesca Young
Jacket Designer Joanne Clark
DTP Designers Nand Kishor Acharya, Sachin Gupta, Vijay Kandwal
Picture Researcher Aditya Katyal
Illustrator Charlotte Ager
Pre-Producer, Pre-Production Dragana Puvacic
Producer Basia Ossowska
Managing Editors Laura Gilbert, Monica Saigal
Deputy Managing Art Editor Ivy Sengupta
Managing Art Editor Diane Peyton Jones
Delhi Team Head Malavika Talukder
Creative Director Helen Senior
Publishing Director Sarah Larter

Subject Consultant Kyair Butts
Literacy Consultant Stephanie Laird

First published in Great Britain in 2019 by
Dorling Kindersley Limited
80 Strand, London, WC2R 0RL
Copyright © 2019 Dorling Kindersley Limited
A Penguin Random House Company
10 9 8 7 6 5 4 3 2
002–308810–Jan/19

All rights reserved.
No part of this publication may be reproduced, stored in or introduced into a retrieval system, or transmitted, in any form, or by any means (electronic, mechanical, photocopying, recording, or otherwise), without the prior written permission of the copyright owner.

A CIP catalogue record for this book
is available from the British Library.
ISBN: 978-0-2413-2288-8

Printed and bound in China

A WORLD OF IDEAS:
SEE ALL THERE IS TO KNOW

www.dk.com

Dear Reader,

I was eight years old when Dr Martin Luther King Jr died – too young to understand fully what had happened, but old enough to know that the United States had lost a great man.

In learning more about Martin's life to write this biography, I finally understood just how great he was. Martin's belief in positive change through love and non-violence made a real difference. When people around him were (understandably) reacting to racism with anger and violence, Martin held firm to his belief that only peaceful action could change the world.

I hope Martin's life will inspire you, as it has inspired me, always to "meet hate with love" and believe in your dreams to create a better world.

Laurie Calkhoven

The life of... Martin **Luther** KING Jr

1
FAMILY OF MINISTERS
page 8

6
THE MOVEMENT SPREADS
page 46

7
"LETTER FROM BIRMINGHAM JAIL"
page 54

8
"I HAVE A DREAM"
page 64

9
SELMA
page 74

2
"WHITES ONLY"
page 16

3
A CLEAR PATH
page 22

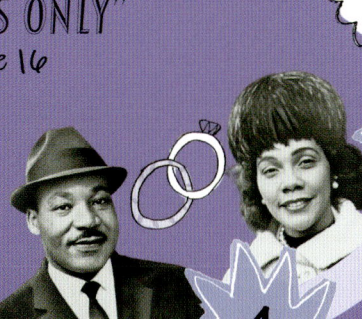

5
ROSA PARKS REFUSES TO STAND
page 36

4
LOVE AND MARRIAGE
page 30

10
THE POVERTY PROBLEM
page 84

11
"FREE AT LAST"
page 92

12
A LASTING LEGACY
page 100

Chapter 1

Family of ministers

Early in his life, there were clues that young Martin Luther King Jr would grow up to become a leader in the fight for civil rights.

Martin was born into a family of clergy. His mother's father, A.D. Williams, was the pastor of Ebenezer Baptist Church in Atlanta, Georgia, USA. Martin's father, Martin Sr, was the church's co-pastor. The Williams and King families lived together in a comfortable house on Auburn Avenue in Atlanta.

Martin Sr, known to his family as "Daddy King", hadn't always lived in Atlanta. He had grown up on a farm in South Georgia where his father was a sharecropper. A sharecropper

What are civil rights? The rights to freedom and equality given by the US Constitution. African-Americans were often denied their civil rights, especially in the South.

is a farmer who works a small plot of land owned by another farmer. In exchange, he gives the landowner some of his crops at the end of the year. Sharecroppers worked very hard, but they barely made enough money to make ends meet.

The King and Williams families lived in this house in Atlanta, Georgia.

One day, Martin Sr saw that the landowner, who was white, was cheating the family out of money his father had earned. He told his father about it right in front of the landowner. The landowner was furious. Martin Sr realized he would have to leave the farm for his own safety and for the safety of his family.

His older sister was living in Atlanta, and he decided to move there, too.

When Martin Sr moved to Atlanta, he wanted to get an education – but there was a problem.

There had been no secondary schools for African-American children in the part of Georgia he was from, so he had not been able to attend one. He finally started secondary school in Atlanta at the age of 18, the age at which most people finish.

He worked hard during the day and went to school at night. Sometimes he fell asleep during a class, but he didn't give up. Martin Sr graduated from school and, later, from Atlanta's Morehouse College.

Atlanta is also where he met and married Alberta Williams, daughter of A.D. Williams. That's when Martin Sr became co-pastor of Ebenezer Baptist Church and a leader in Atlanta's black community.

Life could be hard for black people in the American South. Segregation kept them separated from white people. Black children

---

What is segregation? Keeping people of different races or religions separate from each other, either by law or by other methods.

and white children went to different schools. Black people had to sit at the back of buses and couldn't use public parks or swimming pools. Many shops, hotels, and restaurants were for whites only. Even drinking fountains were separated. Worse, black people were paid less than white people for doing the same jobs.

Martin Sr worked to make life better for people in the black community. He encouraged them to register to vote. He also fought for black teachers to receive the same pay as white teachers.

This is the world that Martin was born into on 15 January 1929. He had an older sister, Christine. He would also have a younger brother,

Alfred Daniel (A.D.). When he was born, Martin was named Michael King, just like his father. It wasn't until he was five years old that "Little Mike" became Martin Luther King Jr. His father changed both of their names from Michael to Martin Luther in honour of a famous religious thinker.

Young Martin was like many other boys. He loved his family and was especially close to his grandmother. He liked to play with his friends. He was good at baseball, and he sang in the church choir.

WHAT'S IN A NAME?

Religious thinker Martin Luther worked to change some basic rules of the Christian church in the 1500s. His work led to the separation between the Roman Catholic Church and the new Protestant churches.

One day, Martin was impressed by a visiting preacher at the church. "Someday I'm going to have me some big words like that," he told his mother.

Martin had high hopes for himself, but it wasn't long before he began to understand the true meaning of signs that read "Whites only". As he grew older, Martin became more and more aware of segregation and the unfair laws, commonly called Jim Crow laws, that separated him from his dreams. Jim Crow laws were named after a character in a travelling show. To play this character, a white actor would blacken his face and sing and dance in a way that made fun of black people.

Many white people in the South wanted to make sure African-Americans would not have the same rights as they did. They passed the Jim Crow laws that separated schools, waiting rooms, and toilets. The laws also forced black people to sit at the back of buses and in separate railway carriages – and, in almost all cases, the spaces for black people were far worse than those reserved for whites.

The Jim Crow laws made life very difficult for black people in the South. Because the laws also made it nearly impossible for them to register to vote, the African-American community had little hope of being able to change things for the better.

Martin Sr graduated from Atlanta's Morehouse College.

Here's Martin.

Martin's family poses for a portrait. At the back, from left to right, are Martin's mother, father, and grandmother. A.D., Christine, and Martin are at the front.

Chapter 2

"Whites only"

Martin's Atlanta neighbourhood was almost entirely African-American. As a boy, his parents protected him from racism – until it was time to start school.

Across the street from the King family's home on Auburn Avenue was a shop that was owned by a white family. Martin and his brother, A.D., would sometimes play with the shop owner's children. When Martin was six years old, shortly after he and his white friend had started at their separate schools, Martin and A.D. crossed the street to find their playmates.

The boys told Martin and A.D. that they couldn't play with them any more because they were Negroes.

WORDS MATTER

When Martin was a boy, "Negro" was the polite term used to refer to African-Americans. Many people, however, used the word "coloured". Others insulted adult men and women by calling them "boy" or "girl" instead of by their names. There were bigger, uglier insults, as well. They were used to make black people feel small.

Martin and his brother were confused and sad. When they told their mother what the shop owner's children had said, she was not surprised. Instead, she explained to them why their family didn't go to the cinema, eat at nice restaurants, or go to the town's best schools.

Mrs King taught her children how to get along in the world of Jim Crow laws, but she also made sure that her children knew those laws were unfair and wrong. "You are as good as anyone," she told Martin.

Martin agreed with his mother. He knew the Jim Crow laws weren't right, and he was going to make a difference. "One day I'm going to turn this world upside down," he promised her.

"One day I'm going to turn this world upside down."

Martin Luther King Jr.

Despite his promise, Martin experienced racism again and again. Once, when Martin was in a department store with his mother, a white woman suddenly slapped him. She yelled and accused him of stepping on her foot. Martin and his mother could do nothing.

Daddy King drove his own car so he wouldn't have to sit at the back of the bus. One day, a police officer pulled him over and said, "Boy, show me your licence." Martin's father pointed to his son and said, "That's a *boy* there. I'm a *man*."

Another time, a shoe-shop worker insisted that Daddy King and Martin move to seats at the back of the shop before he would serve them.

---

what is racism?   The belief that certain people are better or worse than others because of their race. Hating a group of people because of their race is also racism.

"We'll either buy shoes sitting here, or we won't buy any shoes at all," Daddy King said. They left the shop.

When Martin was 14, he travelled to a public-speaking contest with a favourite teacher. Martin's speech, "The Negro and the Constitution", won first prize. In it, he argued that Jim Crow laws were unfair. On the journey home, the bus driver ordered Martin and his teacher to give up their seats to white passengers. Martin was angry, but his teacher convinced him to obey the law. They had to stand for the 145-km (90-mile) trip home. "It was the angriest I have ever been in my life," Martin remembered later.

Despite the racism he experienced, Martin was a successful student. He did extremely well, skipped years, and finished school early.

The summer before going to college, Martin accepted a job at a tobacco farm in Connecticut. It was his

> **DID YOU KNOW?**
> In his speech, Martin said the United States should "give fair play and free opportunity for all people".

first trip north. While there, he saw black and white people working together. He ate at a restaurant and sat right next to a table of white people. He saw what the world could be like without segregation.

Travelling home on the train, he had to change to a "coloured" carriage when they reached Washington, D.C. When he ate in the train's dining carriage, he had to sit behind a curtain. Martin started college determined to make things better for African-Americans, especially in the South.

Chapter 3

A clear path

Martin had been a top student at school. In fact, his grades were so good that he skipped the final year of secondary school.

Because he had skipped another year when he was younger, he started at Morehouse College in 1944 at just 15 years old.

Morehouse was the same college his father and his grandfather had attended. At first, Martin wasn't interested in becoming a minister like the two of them, but he knew that he wanted to serve humanity and the African-American community. He thought he would be able to do that by studying to become a doctor or a lawyer.

In college, Martin joined a group that worked to make black and white people equal in society. He also discovered the work of Henry David Thoreau. Thoreau was a writer who protested against slavery and other injustices in the 1800s with civil disobedience. He refused to pay taxes to a government he thought was unfair and went to jail for his beliefs. By studying Thoreau, Martin realized non-violent protest could change the world.

Henry David Thoreau

At the same time, Martin greatly admired two of his professors, both of whom were ministers. He began to think that by becoming a clergyman, he could do more good in the world than he could as a doctor or a lawyer.

---

what is civil disobedience? When a person uses non-violent, or peaceful, methods when refusing to follow a law they believe to be unjust.

Now Martin had a clear forward path. He would become a Baptist minister and preach about fairness, equality, and peaceful protest.

At 17, Martin gave his first sermon at his father's Ebenezer Baptist Church. Martin started speaking in one of the church's smaller rooms. As he preached, people were drawn to his voice and his message. So many people ended up coming that the sermon had to be moved to the church's main auditorium. It was a very powerful talk. Church members who had watched Martin grow up suddenly saw him as a man instead of a boy.

Daddy King would have been happy for Martin to join him as assistant pastor as soon as he graduated from college, but Martin wanted more education – so, at 19, he travelled north to Crozer Theological Seminary in Pennsylvania.

Martin would give many sermons at Ebenezer Baptist Church throughout his life. This picture is of him preaching there in 1960.

At Crozer, Martin was just one of a few black students in a class of about a hundred. Martin knew that some white people, even in the north, had negative images of black people. He made sure he worked hard and was always on time for classes. He was also always well dressed. He liked snazzy sports jackets, two-tone shoes, and tweed suits so much that his classmates at Morehouse gave him a nickname – "Tweed".

Martin read the works of many different philosophers, and he began to believe even more strongly in Thoreau's ideas about non-violent protest. He wondered, though, if it would truly be possible to solve all the problems of segregation without resorting to violence.

That changed when Martin discovered the work of Mohandas

Gandhi. Gandhi, an Indian leader, had won his country's freedom from an unfair government, and he had done so using non-violent protest.

Gandhi, Martin wrote in a tribute to him, "resisted with love instead of hate". Martin's study of Gandhi made him believe that he could confront the evils of segregation and racism with the same non-violent methods.

INSPIRING LEADER

Mohandas Gandhi was an Indian activist and leader. He played a big role in helping India gain its independence from Great Britain in the 1930s and 1940s. He also fought for the rights of India's poor. Gandhi's non-violent methods inspired movements for civil rights and freedom around the world. He is often called "Mahatma", a title given to people who are very wise and holy.

Martin graduated from Crozer at the top of his class in 1951 and won a scholarship to continue his studies. Daddy King was so proud of his son that he gave Martin a brand-new green Chevrolet as a graduation gift. Martin drove this car north to Boston, Massachusetts, where he could get his doctoral degree at Boston University.

It was in Boston that he met the woman who would help him change the world – Coretta Scott.

Martin and his sister celebrate their graduations in 1948. Martin graduated from Morehouse College, and Christine graduated from Spelman College.

Chapter

Love AND marriage

Even though Martin had moved even further north, he still found racism in Boston. Fortunately he found Coretta there, too.

"I went into place after place where there were signs that rooms were for rent," Martin later remembered about looking for a home in Boston. "They were for rent until they found out I was a Negro, and suddenly they had just been rented."

Martin eventually found a place to live and focused on his studies. He continued to think about how he could do the most good in the world. He had come to believe that non-violent resistance was the strongest weapon available in the search for civil rights.

But Martin did more than just study in Boston. He began to think about finding a wife.

A friend gave Martin the phone number of Coretta Scott, a student at Boston's New England Conservatory of Music. Coretta wanted to be a singer and to teach music. Like Martin, she was from the South – in her case, Alabama.

Coretta Scott

Martin called Coretta and asked her to have lunch with him. At lunch they talked about everything from southern soul food and music to segregation and racial injustice in the South. From their very first meeting, Martin could tell that Coretta was just as dedicated as he was to the idea of change.

"After an hour, my mind was made up," Martin remembered later. Before lunch was over, he said, "We ought to get married someday."

Daddy King had always wanted Martin to come back to Atlanta, become co-pastor of Ebenezer Baptist Church, and marry an Atlanta girl. He tried to discourage the romance. But the more time Martin spent with Coretta, the more sure he was that he wanted to marry her.

On 18 June 1953, the young couple were married in the front garden of Coretta's family home in Alabama by Daddy King. No hotels in the area would rent a room to black people, so the couple spent their honeymoon night in the guest room of family friends. Those friends just happened to live in a funeral parlour!

Martin and Coretta spent the rest of the summer in Atlanta and then drove back to Boston to finish their studies.

"TO LOVE, HONOUR, AND OBEY"

At the time Coretta married Martin, most brides promised "to love, honour, and obey" their husbands. Grooms were not expected to promise to obey their wives. Coretta said that she would not promise to obey. Daddy King was shocked, but he agreed to leave the word out of their wedding vows.

Martin and Coretta smile on their wedding day in 1953.

Martin had a number of choices as to where he would work when he graduated. Three colleges had offered him positions. Two churches in the north wanted him to become their minister. Daddy King hoped Martin and Coretta would come home to Atlanta. Then a church in Montgomery, Alabama – the Dexter Avenue Baptist Church – invited Martin to come down south and preach.

In January 1954, Martin drove from Boston to Montgomery to visit the church. Martin knew that if the church members liked his sermon, he would be asked to become their permanent minister. His sermons were always powerful. They made people think, and they made people want to change the world for the better. The sermon he delivered as a guest preacher that Sunday was no different and, of course, he was offered the job.

Martin and Coretta knew life in the north would be easier for them. Going back down south meant living under Jim Crow

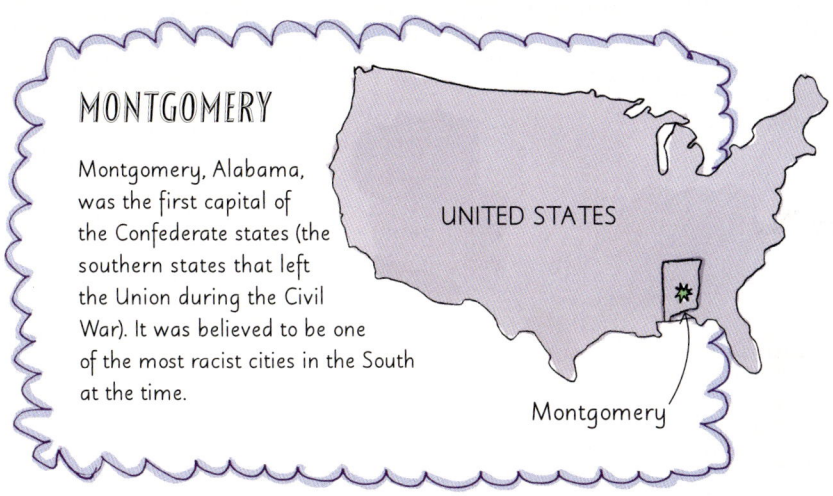

MONTGOMERY

Montgomery, Alabama, was the first capital of the Confederate states (the southern states that left the Union during the Civil War). It was believed to be one of the most racist cities in the South at the time.

UNITED STATES

Montgomery

laws again. It meant having to sit at the back of the bus. It meant being called names like "boy". But the South was also their home.

Martin and Coretta decided to go where they thought they could do the most good, so they made the hard decision to move to Montgomery. On 1 September 1954, they moved into their new home. They found themselves settling into new jobs, a new house, and a new city all at the same time – and soon they would also find themselves in the middle of a movement to change the world.

Chapter 5

Rosa Parks REFUSES TO STAND

Martin preached about the need to change the world for the better, and his actions matched his words.

As soon as he moved to Montgomery, Martin joined the Montgomery chapter of the National Association for the Advancement of Colored People (NAACP). He asked the members of 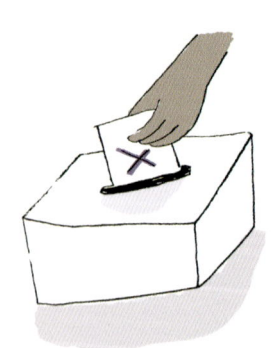 his new church to become members of the NAACP as well. He also told them how important it was that they register to vote. Voting lets people show politicians what they believe in. Martin knew that voting is the way to make changes happen in a community, state, or country.

Martin and Coretta had been in Montgomery for little more than a year when their first child, a daughter they named Yolanda, was born. Then, just three weeks later, on 1 December 1955, a seamstress called Rosa Parks refused to give up her seat on a Montgomery bus.

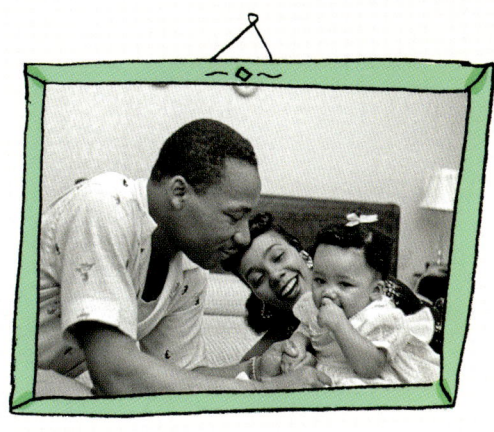

Martin, Coretta, and baby Yolanda at home in May 1956.

The bus system in Montgomery was segregated by law. Black people had to sit at the back of the bus while white people sat at the front. If more white passengers got on the bus, black passengers were expected to give up their seats and stand.

TERRIBLE TRICK

Black people had to pay their fares at the front of the bus, then walk around the outside of the bus to the back door. Sometimes white bus drivers would drive off without them after they had paid, just for fun.

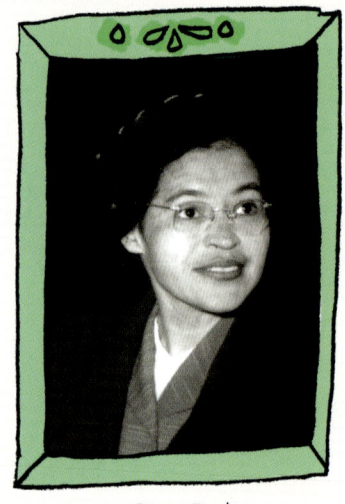
Rosa Parks

Rosa Parks, who had been a secretary for the NAACP, decided she had had enough. One night after work, a bus driver ordered her to give up her seat for a white man. Parks refused. She was arrested.

Martin held a meeting with Montgomery's black civic leaders and the ministers at his church. They agreed it was time to protest about their unfair treatment with a bus boycott. They worked all weekend to get the word out to the black community.

On Monday 5 December, Martin and Coretta got up early to watch the first bus drive past the stop in front of their house. There was not one person on that normally crowded bus!

What is a boycott? When people refuse to deal with a person or an organization as a way of protesting.

Martin drove around the city to see what was happening. Men and women were walking to work. Students were walking to school. The pavements were busy, but the buses were empty.

The first day of the boycott was a huge success. That night, black leaders formed the Montgomery Improvement Association to lead the boycott. They made Martin their president.

City leaders were unhappy. They ordered taxis to charge higher fares to try to force people back on the buses. The community organized shared cars instead, and then the city tried to put a stop to those, too. Martin urged everyone to stay strong and remember their protest was non-violent. He got hate mail and nasty phone calls from the Ku Klux Klan (KKK), but he didn't back down.

One night, Martin was at a meeting when someone threw a firebomb onto his front porch. He rushed home to make sure Coretta and Yolanda were safe. Luckily they had been at the back of the house. People gathered around the house. They were angry, and they

HATEFUL GROUP

The Ku Klux Klan, or KKK, is a hate group. The KKK was formed after the American Civil War and was active in almost every southern US state. Its members used violence and murder to frighten black people and to keep them from taking leading roles in society.

wanted justice. Martin knew that things could quickly become out of control.

He walked out onto the porch, held up his hand for silence, and began to speak. "We must meet hate with love," he told the crowd, and he asked them to keep faith that the boycott would work. His inspiring words prevented what could have turned into a riot.

"We must meet hate with love."

Martin Luther King Jr, 1956

When Montgomery's government declared the bus boycott illegal, its organizers weren't intimidated or scared. People began showing up at the jail, turning themselves in for boycotting.

Television news cameras were filming when Martin left the courtroom where he had been convicted of violating the law and ordered to pay a $500 fine. Suddenly, Martin and the boycott were national news.

While all of this was happening, Martin and the Montgomery Improvement Association had taken their case to the US Supreme Court.

What is the Supreme Court? The highest court in the United States. It is one of the three branches of government established by the US Constitution.

On 15 November 1956, nearly a full year after the boycott had begun, the US Supreme Court declared that the laws forcing black passengers to ride at the back of the bus were unconstitutional.

A few weeks later, on 21 December 1956, integrated buses began running. Martin waited at the bus stop in front of his house, and when the bus came, he got on and sat in the front seat. The Montgomery bus boycott had ended in success, and a new freedom movement was born. Martin would soon be called upon to be its leader.

African-Americans in Montgomery walk to work during the bus boycott. They disapproved of the unfair laws.

After the Supreme Court's ruling, Martin waits with friends to board a newly desegregated bus.

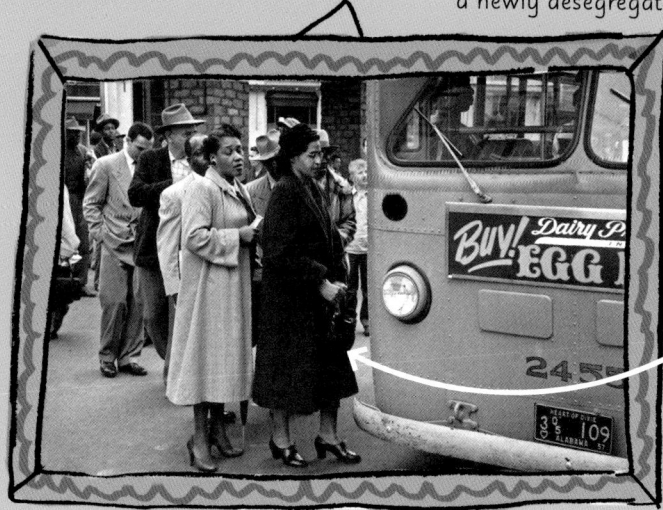

Here's Rosa.

Rosa Parks is one of the first people onto the bus once the boycott is over. What began with her refusal to give up her seat had ended in success.

Chapter 6

THE movement SPREADS

Integrating the buses in Montgomery had been a success. The boycott brought national attention to Martin and his cause.

Martin and other black ministers met in Atlanta to talk about their next move. They decided to form an organization – the Southern Christian Leadership Conference, or SCLC – dedicated to integration and the fight for civil rights. Martin was named their chairman. He travelled around the country giving speeches, and he even made the cover of *Time* magazine in February 1957.

While Martin was travelling around the country, Coretta was often at home alone with

---

What is integration?   Bringing people from different races together to make sure that they have equal rights.

Yolanda, and later with Martin Luther King III, who was born in October 1957.

Over the next two years, people in the South worked to integrate schools. In the 1954 case of Brown v. Board of Education, the Supreme Court had ruled that segregated schools were unequal and against the law. Despite the ruling, many white southerners still had a one-word answer to the idea of integrated schools – "Never!"

COURAGEOUS STUDENTS

In 1957, nine black students enrolled in Little Rock Central High School in Little Rock, Arkansas. On their first day, the students were met with angry white protestors, and the governor of Arkansas wouldn't allow them in. President Eisenhower sent soldiers to make sure the students could enter the school. The soldiers guarded them for the entire school year, but they couldn't protect them from the ugly things white students said. It was the start of a long, painful process of integrating schools in the South.

Martin knew the fight for integration would be a long one, and he wanted to learn even more about non-violent protest in order to win it. In 1959, he and Coretta travelled to India. They walked in the footsteps of Gandhi, and came home believing even more strongly in peaceful protest.

The demands of the freedom movement made it impossible for Martin to be a full-time pastor in Montgomery. After returning from India, the family moved to Atlanta, where Martin would share duties with Daddy King at Ebenezer Baptist Church.

Black students in the South had been holding non-violent protests of their own. They said it was unfair that they could shop in stores, but that those same stores wouldn't serve them at their lunch counters. On 1 February 1960, four college students in Greensboro, North Carolina, sat down at a Woolworth lunch

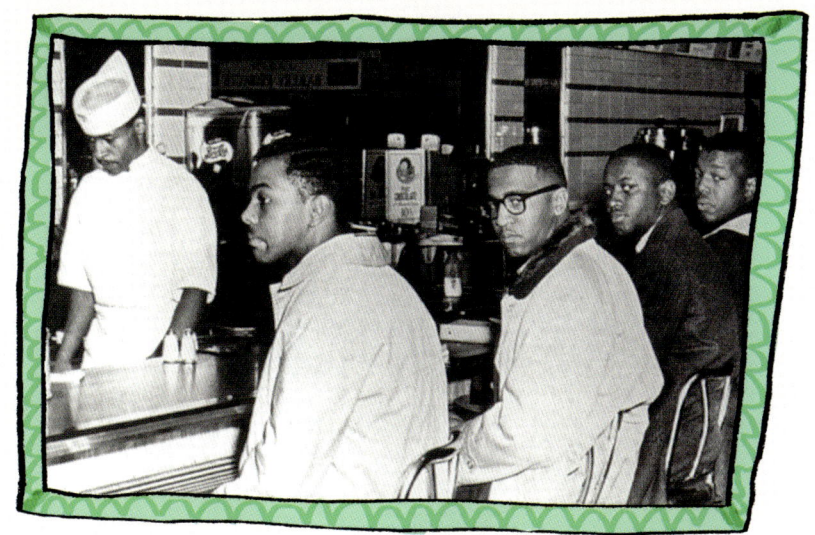

Woolworth department store lunch counter, Greensboro.

counter and tried to order. "We don't serve coloured here," they were told. The men sat quietly until the shop closed. The next day, even more students showed up.

In cities across the South, college students held sit-ins at lunch counters, cinemas, and parks. They were shouted at, beaten, and had food thrown at them, but the students didn't react. Instead, they formed the Student Nonviolent Coordinating Committee (SNCC).

| What is a sit-in? | A protest in which people sit in one place and refuse to leave until they are forced to, or given what they demand. |

Martin is handcuffed and brought to court after his arrest in 1960.

In October 1960, the SNCC asked Martin to join a protest in Atlanta. Martin walked into the department store and sat at the "Whites only" lunch counter. He and 75 students were arrested for trespassing. Five days later, they were released from jail after the store owners dropped the charges – but Martin was arrested again on a fake traffic violation and sentenced to four months in Georgia State Prison.

Martin's supporters contacted the two men who were running for president at the time, John F. Kennedy and Richard M. Nixon. Nixon made no comment, but Kennedy called Coretta and said he would do what he could. Soon Martin was released on bail.

On the Sunday before Election Day, black ministers across the country spoke out in favour of Kennedy. In one of the closest elections in United States history, Kennedy won the presidency.

John F. Kennedy

DID YOU KNOW?

The Woolworth lunch counter where the students held their first sit-in is now at the Smithsonian Museum of American History in Washington, D.C.

The student sit-ins at lunch counters had been successful. Store owners lost so much business that they agreed to serve black people alongside white people. However, many other places were still segregated. Martin met the new president, John F. Kennedy, and his brother, Attorney General Robert F. Kennedy, to talk about a civil rights bill to end segregation in the United States once and for all.

The civil rights bill was on a long list of things Kennedy wanted to do, but it wasn't very high on that list. As the Kings welcomed their third child, Dexter, in January 1961, Martin thought about how to get President Kennedy to pay attention.

People wait at a segregated lunch counter in 1960. Sit-ins and "stand-in-line" protests forced businesses to reconsider their rules.

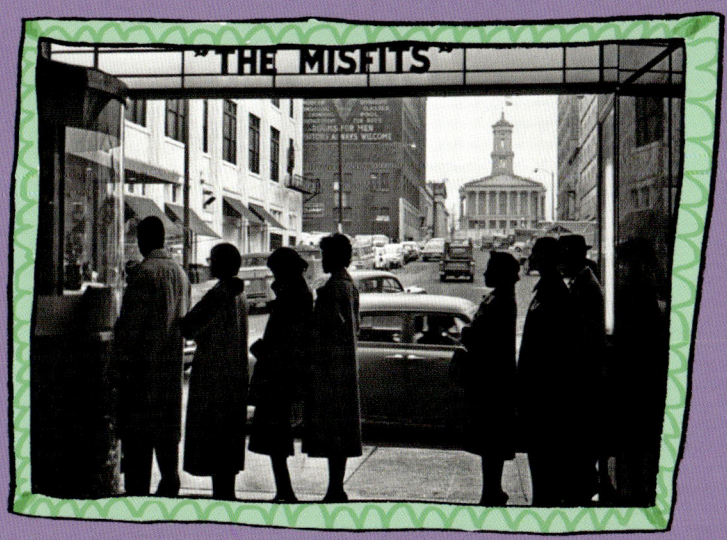

A "stand-in-line" protest takes place at a cinema in Nashville, Tennessee. About 300 people protested at Nashville cinemas in 1961 by waiting in line and refusing to leave.

Chapter 7

"Letter FROM BIRMINGHAM JAIL"

The Civil Rights Movement had made great progress by 1961, but there was still a long way to go.

A group of black and white students called Freedom Riders decided to travel south to test a federal law that said places like bus and train stations could no longer be segregated. On the way down, one of their buses was firebombed outside Birmingham, Alabama. When the students ran off the bus, the attackers beat them with baseball bats and chains. More students arrived to keep the Freedom Rides going. Their protests were peaceful, but they were often met with violence and arrests.

Martin flew to Montgomery to talk to a group of Freedom Riders. An angry mob threw rocks and tear gas around the church where they were meeting. Martin got in touch with Robert F. Kennedy, who sent soldiers from the National Guard to protect the Freedom Riders and their supporters.

One city that refused to give up its "Whites only" waiting room was Albany, Georgia. When SNCC students tried to make the train station end its segregation policy, they were thrown into jail. In response, Martin organized and led a

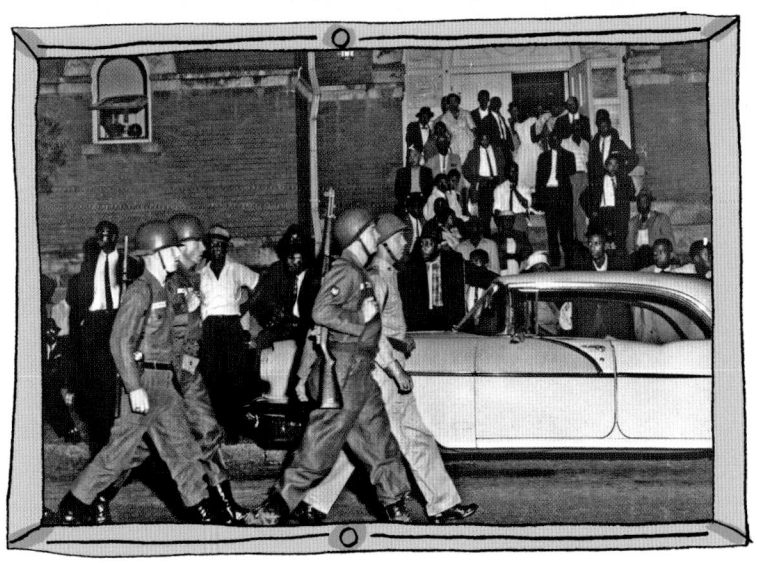

National Guard soldiers come to Alabama to help protect the Freedom Riders on 22 May 1961.

peaceful protest march through the city, singing "We Shall Overcome". He was arrested. More people protested. More people were imprisoned.

One night, a woman was beaten when she tried to bring food into the jail. The black community couldn't contain its anger, and a riot broke out. Martin left the city. He felt as if his time in Albany had been a failure.

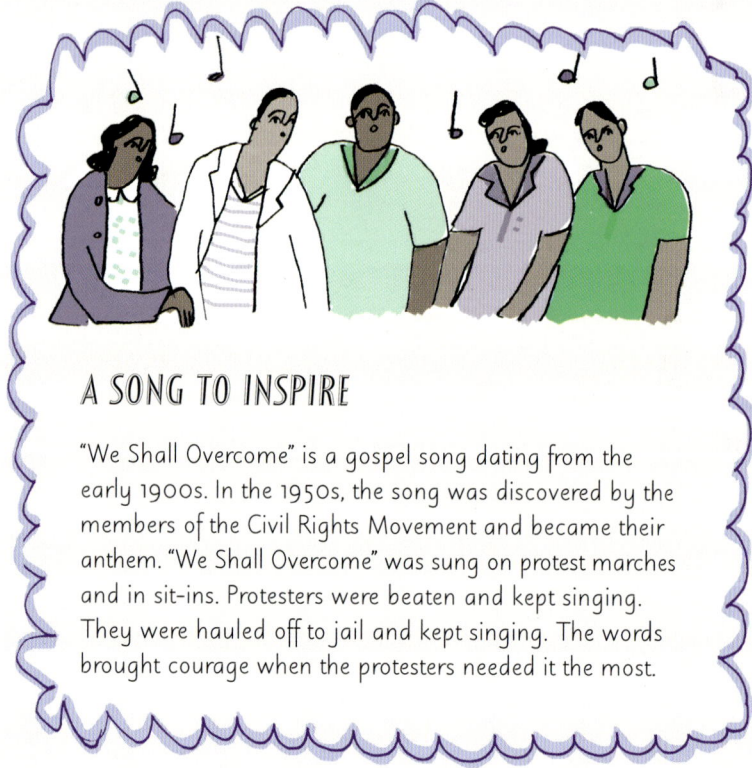

A SONG TO INSPIRE

"We Shall Overcome" is a gospel song dating from the early 1900s. In the 1950s, the song was discovered by the members of the Civil Rights Movement and became their anthem. "We Shall Overcome" was sung on protest marches and in sit-ins. Protesters were beaten and kept singing. They were hauled off to jail and kept singing. The words brought courage when the protesters needed it the most.

"Oh, down in my **heart**, I do **believe** we'll **overcome** some day."

"We Shall Overcome"

When Bernice was born in 1963, Martin's family was complete. This family portrait of Martin, Coretta, and their four children was taken four years later, in 1967.

Martin was thinking about the next move for the freedom movement when his fourth child, Bernice, was born in 1963. After some time at home with his family, he and the other SCLC leaders decided to make the city of Birmingham, Alabama, their focus.

Birmingham's Commissioner for Public Safety, Eugene "Bull" Connor, had done nothing while Freedom Riders were bombed and beaten. He was against the Civil Rights Movement and had no interest in helping anyone fighting for equality. To combat this, the SCLC launched Project C. The C was for "confrontation".

Project C targeted "Whites only" lunch counters at three stores in the city. Black students sat at the counters and refused to move. Twenty-one people were arrested on the first day. The next day, more members of Martin's "non-violent army" arrived to take their places – and the next day, and the next. In all, hundreds were arrested. Shop owners were upset about the business they were losing.

A state court ordered an end to the demonstrations. Instead, Martin led a march. He was arrested and thrown into jail.

Martin was kept in solitary confinement, meaning he was isolated from the other

What is confrontation? A meeting in which people challenge, or confront, one another, usually in an angry way.

> **DID YOU KNOW?**
>
> Martin wrote his "Letter from Birmingham Jail" on the edges of a newspaper and on toilet paper.

prisoners. He wasn't even allowed anything to read, but a friend smuggled in a newspaper. In the newspaper, he read that white ministers were asking him to stop his protest. Martin's lawyers smuggled a pen into the jail for him, and with that pen, he wrote something that would become famous – his "Letter from Birmingham Jail".

When he was released, Martin saw protestors were getting discouraged. Many were still in jail.

"LETTER FROM BIRMINGHAM JAIL"

Some white ministers in Birmingham asked the black community not to support the SCLC's efforts. From his cell, Martin wrote a letter that would be published in newspapers across the country. He defended the non-violent demonstrations as a necessary step to create change. "We will reach the goal of freedom in Birmingham and all over the nation, because the goal of America is freedom," he wrote.

Young protestors show their support for integration during the Children's Crusade. They knew they were likely to be arrested.

Others needed to work to feed their families. The movement turned to a new source of protesters – children. On 2 May 1963, the Children's Crusade began. More than 1,000 college, secondary school, and even primary school students began a march from the 16th Street Baptist Church. Many were arrested. The next day, more arrived to take their place.

Bull Connor demanded the students turn back. They refused, so he told his police and firefighters to let the children have it. Police dogs lunged at them, and firefighters turned their powerful water hoses on them. News cameras captured it all.

Day after day, the children kept coming. Finally, the firefighters refused to attack them any more. They were impressed by the children's bravery.

On 10 May 1963 – 38 days after Project C began – an agreement was reached with the city's businesses. They could hold out no longer – integration would finally come to Birmingham.

That night, a bomb exploded outside Martin's hotel room. He had already left the city and was unharmed, but he returned to Birmingham to stop the riots that broke out.

The riots made President Kennedy see that a civil rights bill was needed. He urged Congress to get to work. Martin and the other leaders wanted to make sure Congress listened. They planned a march on Washington, D.C., to show the world how much they needed freedom.

"It ought to be possible... for every **American** to enjoy the **privileges** of being American **without** regard to his **race** or his **colour**."

John F. Kennedy,
11 June 1963

Chapter 8

"I have a **dream**"

The night President Kennedy told Congress a civil rights bill was long overdue, a black leader named Medgar Evers was shot and killed.

The shooting took place in Jackson, the capital city of Mississippi. The shooter was a white supremacist, which is a person who believes that white people are better than black people and all other races.

MEDGAR EVERS

Evers wasn't allowed to vote when he came home from World War II. In response, he organized local chapters of the NAACP and travelled all over Mississippi to lead voter registration drives. In Jackson, he fought to end segregation and to open up good jobs to African-Americans.

The black community was sad and angry. Martin was sad and angry, too. He knew that he would have to keep the pressure on Congress to make sure a civil rights bill was passed. He and the SCLC planned a march to prove just how many people supported equal rights for African-Americans.

More than 250,000 people of all different races travelled from every state in the USA to participate in the March on Washington for Jobs and Freedom on 28 August 1963. They travelled by car and bus. They travelled by plane. A few even walked all the way from New York City. They came to show their government and the rest of the country that the Jim Crow laws had to go.

Many government leaders, including Robert F. Kennedy, said they feared that there would be violence. The protestors proved them wrong. They peacefully marched from the Washington Monument to the Lincoln Memorial, singing "We Shall Overcome" all the way. When they arrived at the Lincoln Memorial, the crowd gathered to hear speeches.

Religious leaders and members of different civil rights groups gave inspiring speeches, and well-known singers such as Marian Anderson, Joan Baez, and Bob Dylan led everyone in the national anthem and other songs. However, it was Martin's speech that meant the most to the crowd. It has since been named one of the greatest speeches in American history.

Martin told the marchers that he had a dream. He described a world in which people of all colours were not only equal, but also loved one another. He shared a dream of the sons of former slaves and the sons of former slave owners sitting down together at the table of brotherhood.

"I have a dream that my four little children will one day live in a nation where they will not be judged by the colour of their skin but by the content of their character. I have a dream today!"

He finished by saying that only when the country "let freedom ring", from every state, city, village, and hamlet, would people truly be free.

The march and especially Martin's speech made national news. His words inspired the entire country and even the world. It was one of the greatest moments of the Civil Rights Movement, and people everywhere were optimistic that freedom and equality would surely follow.

Martin addresses the large crowd gathered to hear his speech at the 1963 March on Washington.

Just two weeks later, on 15 September 1963, Martin was preaching his Sunday sermon at the Ebenezer Baptist Church when he learned that a bomb had gone off in Birmingham.

Four members of the Ku Klux Klan had set off sticks of dynamite at the 16th Street Baptist Church, the church that had been a gathering place for marchers during the Birmingham protests earlier that year. Twenty-two people were injured in the terrible attack. Even worse, three 14-year-old girls and one 11-year-old girl who had been attending Sunday school that day were killed.

The 16th Street Baptist Church is still an active church. It was named a National Historic Landmark in 2006.

Martin flew to Birmingham to try to keep riots from breaking out, but the murder of four young girls made many people wonder if non-violence was still the way to go. Some believed that it was time to start fighting for their rights with the same violent tactics that were being used against them. Martin urged his followers to continue to be peaceful. He never stopped believing that non-violence was the only way to change the world.

> **DID YOU KNOW?**
>
> In 2013, President Obama awarded a medal in honour of the four girls killed in 1963.

Violence shook the country again on the afternoon of 22 November 1963. President Kennedy was shot and killed in Dallas, Texas. Martin was sad to lose the man who had been a friend to the Civil Rights Movement and to Martin himself.

With Kennedy's death, his vice president – Lyndon B. Johnson – became the new president of the United States.

LYNDON B. JOHNSON

The 36th US president, Johnson grew up poor, without electricity or running water. He worked with Congress to pass laws inspired by Kennedy and his own War on Poverty.

Five days later, President Johnson spoke to Congress. In his speech, he said that the best way to honour President Kennedy's memory was to pass the Civil Rights Bill.

On 2 July 1964, Martin was standing behind President Johnson when he signed the Civil Rights Act. The act made discrimination in public places and businesses illegal. It also made it possible for the government to force public schools to end segregation.

It was a step forwards for civil rights. Making sure black people had the right to vote, however, was something that Martin would have to continue fighting for.

Martin looks on as President Johnson signs the Civil Rights Act of 1964.

Chapter 9

Selma

The March on Washington and the passing of the Civil Rights Act of 1964 were victories for Martin and African-Americans all over the country.

Martin's strong words had inspired many people. At the end of the year, he discovered that he was the winner of the Nobel Peace Prize. In his acceptance speech, he announced that he would share the prize and the prize money with the Civil Rights Movement. "I still believe that we shall overcome," he declared. "This faith can give us courage to face the uncertainties of the future."

What is the Nobel Peace Prize? A medal given each year to a person or group who has worked for world peace. Nobel prizes are also given for chemistry, physics, medicine, and literature.

FREEDOM SUMMER

During the summer of 1964, thousands of northern college students, many of them white, went down south to encourage African-Americans to register to vote. The students also set up Freedom Schools to prepare voters for the difficult tests they would have to pass in order to register. The students were often beaten and jailed for their efforts. Three of them were killed by the KKK in Mississippi.

Throughout 1964 the Student Nonviolent Coordinating Committee (SNCC) had been working in Selma, Alabama, to register black voters, with little success. Part of the problem was that a state judge had made it illegal for black people to hold group meetings. Another part of the problem was the local sheriff, Jim Clark. He said that any black person who tried to vote would be beaten with clubs and cattle prods. The city's black leaders turned to Martin and the SCLC for help. Martin answered their call and arrived in Selma in January 1965.

DID YOU KNOW?

More than half of Selma's citizens were black, but less than one per cent of them were registered to vote.

On 18 January 1965, 50 African-Americans marched as a group to the courthouse to register to vote. They were arrested. Over and over again, more people marched to the court, only to be arrested. Each time, Sheriff Clark met the groups wearing a pin on his uniform that read, "Never".

On 1 February, Martin gathered 700 supporters and marched to the courthouse. He was arrested and imprisoned, which made headlines across the country.

More and more people kept marching in Selma and in other counties in Alabama, too. A group of 105 black teachers marched, even though they knew that their white school board might fire them for doing so. In another march, a young man was shot and killed by a state trooper while he was trying to protect his mother from being beaten.

People dance during the civil rights protests in Selma. They also marched and chanted to show their support for voting rights.

Protesters link arms and sing outside the Dallas Country Courthouse in Selma. Many of them were later arrested.

MALCOLM X

Malcolm X, a black leader and powerful speaker, disagreed with Martin's belief in non-violence. He thought they should be fighting violence with violence. He urged African-Americans to be proud of their heritage, and instead of integration, he wanted the races to be separate. Despite their differences, Martin and Malcolm X respected each other. Martin was deeply sad when Malcolm X was killed in 1965.

While Martin was in jail, the SNCC invited Malcolm X to speak in Selma. Malcolm X and Martin had very different views, and Martin was afraid the people would turn to violence. He organized a peaceful march as a way to make sure that wouldn't happen.

The march would begin in Selma and end in Montgomery, an 87-km (54-mile) walk that would show the nation that African-Americans in the South needed voting rights, and they needed them now. Alabama's governor, George Wallace, said the march could not take place.

Martin was preaching in Atlanta on 7 March 1965, when 600 people gathered to begin their march. As they crossed over the Edmund Pettus Bridge, Alabama state troopers were waiting. The marchers were met with violence and tear gas. The news coverage shocked the nation. More than 70 marchers had to be hospitalized, and many more had minor injuries. The day came to be known as Bloody Sunday.

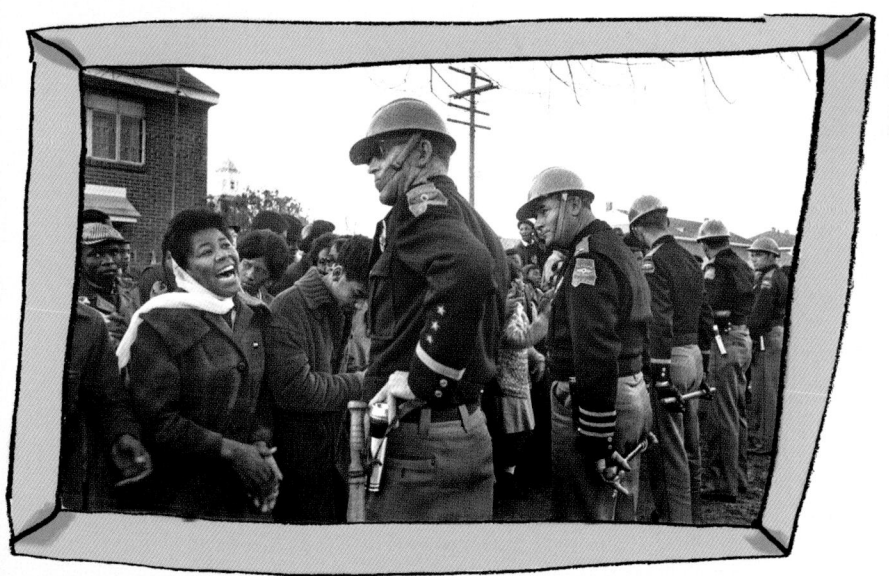

Protesters encounter the waiting Alabama state troopers on their march from Selma to Montgomery in 1965.

Martin asked religious leaders to support the marchers. People from all over the country came to Selma, including white ministers, priests, and rabbis. They gathered to march again a few days later, but a federal judge had banned their protest. Although Martin had never ignored a federal court order, he felt the need to gather anyway – "because our nation has a date with destiny," he said.

When they reached the bridge and were ordered to stop, Martin and the others knelt to pray. Then they turned around and went back to Selma until they could be heard by a federal judge and given permission to march.

That night, three white ministers were walking home from dinner when they were beaten by members of the KKK. One of the ministers, James Reeb, was killed.

There was a national uproar. President Johnson addressed Congress on television and asked for a voting rights bill.

A federal judge ruled that the people had the constitutional right to march from Selma to Montgomery. On Sunday 21 March, more than 3,000 people gathered. They were protected from violence by the National Guard. By the time they reached Montgomery five days later, their number had increased to 25,000 people.

On 6 August 1965, President Johnson signed the Voting Rights Act. This new law banned the difficult tests and other means the southern states had been using to keep black people from voting. By the following summer, 9,000 African-Americans were registered to vote in Selma.

Holding hands, Martin and Coretta lead more than 3,000 marchers across the Edmund Pettis Bridge in Selma. The five-day voting rights march to the capital in Montgomery proved to the world that peaceful protest could win the day.

Chapter 10

THE poverty PROBLEM

By 1965, 10 years after the Montgomery bus boycott, the Civil Rights Movement had seen many successes.

Black people could vote. They could sit anywhere they wanted to on buses and eat at any lunch counter. However, many lived in crime-filled slums and still didn't have good jobs. Inner-city schools were often falling apart and didn't have enough teachers. Frustrated children dropped out of school, giving them little hope for a better future. Despite the Civil Rights Movement's successes, black people were struggling, and the cause of their struggles was poverty.

What is a slum? A poor, crowded, and dirty section of a city. A slum in which people of one race or religious group live is called a ghetto.

This was true of African-Americans all over the country, not just in the South. Cities like New York, Los Angeles, and Chicago were among the worst.

In August 1965, the same month the Voting Rights Act was signed, angry and frustrated people started a riot in the black neighbourhood of Watts in Los Angeles, California. A black man had been arrested by white police officers for what the crowd believed was a made-up traffic charge. The riot lasted for six days and led to riots in other cities. Martin began to see that as long as black people lived in poverty, in northern as well as southern states, they could never be truly free.

Martin and his fellow marchers link arms to show unity as they march to Chicago's City Hall in July 1965.

The riots in Los Angeles and other cities convinced Martin that he had to do more to fight poverty. He visited slums in New York City and Massachusetts. In July 1965, Martin was asked to lead a march in Chicago from the black ghetto to City Hall. He saw that most black people living in the city were poor, with low-paying jobs or no jobs at all. There were laws against segregation, but that didn't stop white landlords from refusing to rent houses and apartments to black families.

In 1966, Martin, Coretta, and their four children moved to Chicago. Martin felt that he needed to live among the people he was trying to help. They lived in a run-down, two-bedroom flat in a black neighbourhood. There were no parks nearby for the children to play in. Their rent was $90 a month. A nicer apartment in a poor white neighbourhood cost $10 less, but most of the white landlords there wouldn't have rented to the King family.

Martin criticized Chicago's white leaders, especially Mayor Richard J. Daley, for not doing enough to help Chicago's poor.

Mayor Daley wasn't happy with Martin's attention. He had tried to keep Chicago's black residents on his side with weak promises to clean up the ghettos, but the community was restless. They wanted change, and they weren't ready to commit to non-violence.

Richard J. Daley

Daley was the mayor of Chicago from 1955 until he died in 1976. He was considered to be the last of the big-city "bosses", mayors who kept a tight control on their cities by giving government jobs to their supporters. Daley was powerful, but he did little to end segregation.

Soon Martin realized the movement faced an even bigger problem. President Johnson was turning his attention to the Vietnam War.

WAR IN VIETNAM

US soldiers went to South Vietnam, in Asia, to help its democratic government beat the communists in North Vietnam. Many Americans, Martin included, spoke against the war. The USA pulled its soldiers out of the country in 1973, and it fell to the communists two years later.

Vietnam War protests took place across the US. This flier is for one in New York.

NEW YORK

MOBILIZE TO STOP THE WAR IN VIETNAM

Saturday, April 15.

Assemble 11 a.m.
Central Park Sheep Meadow (66 St.)
March at noon to the United Nations.

Antiwar protests were taking place all over the United States. The Civil Rights Movement was being pushed aside in the face of these other worries.

Young leaders in the movement had very different views about its future. Some of them carried guns. They thought it might be time to fight back against beatings at the hands of white police officers. Martin believed they were wrong. He never stopped believing that peaceful resistance was better and more effective than violence.

He worried that young black men who had few opportunities at home were being sent thousands of miles away to Vietnam to fight for the rights of others. He spoke out against the war, something that made President Johnson unhappy. Many years before, President Kennedy had warned Martin that the FBI was keeping an eye on him. Now they were watching him even more closely.

With violence at home on the rise and attention in Congress turned to the war, Martin tried to keep his non-violent movement in people's minds. In 1967, he published a new book, called *Where Do We Go From Here: Chaos or Community?* In it, he urged people of all races to work together to bring an end to racism and poverty. Unless everyone participated in the movement, he argued, true change would never come.

After the book was published, Martin decided to stage another march on the nation's capital in the spring of 1968. He wanted to bring people of all races together to demonstrate for better jobs and higher pay. Martin called this project the Poor People's Campaign.

"No **great** victories are **won** in a war for the **transformation** of a whole people without **total** participation."

Martin Luther King, Jr,
Where Do We Go From Here: Chaos or Community?, 1967

Chapter 11

"Free at last"

Martin was busy organizing his Poor People's Campaign in Chicago when he got an urgent call for help.

Black sanitation workers (rubbish collectors) in Memphis, Tennessee, were on strike. They had started a union, which is an organized group of workers. The union had been trying to get better working conditions and fair pay for its members. The city leaders had said no.

The strikers marched every day wearing signs that read, "I AM A MAN". They wanted respect, and they wanted fairness. Instead, they were beaten by police. Then the authorities got a judge to order the marches to stop.

| What is a strike? | When workers refuse to work in order to convince or force their employer to meet their demands. |

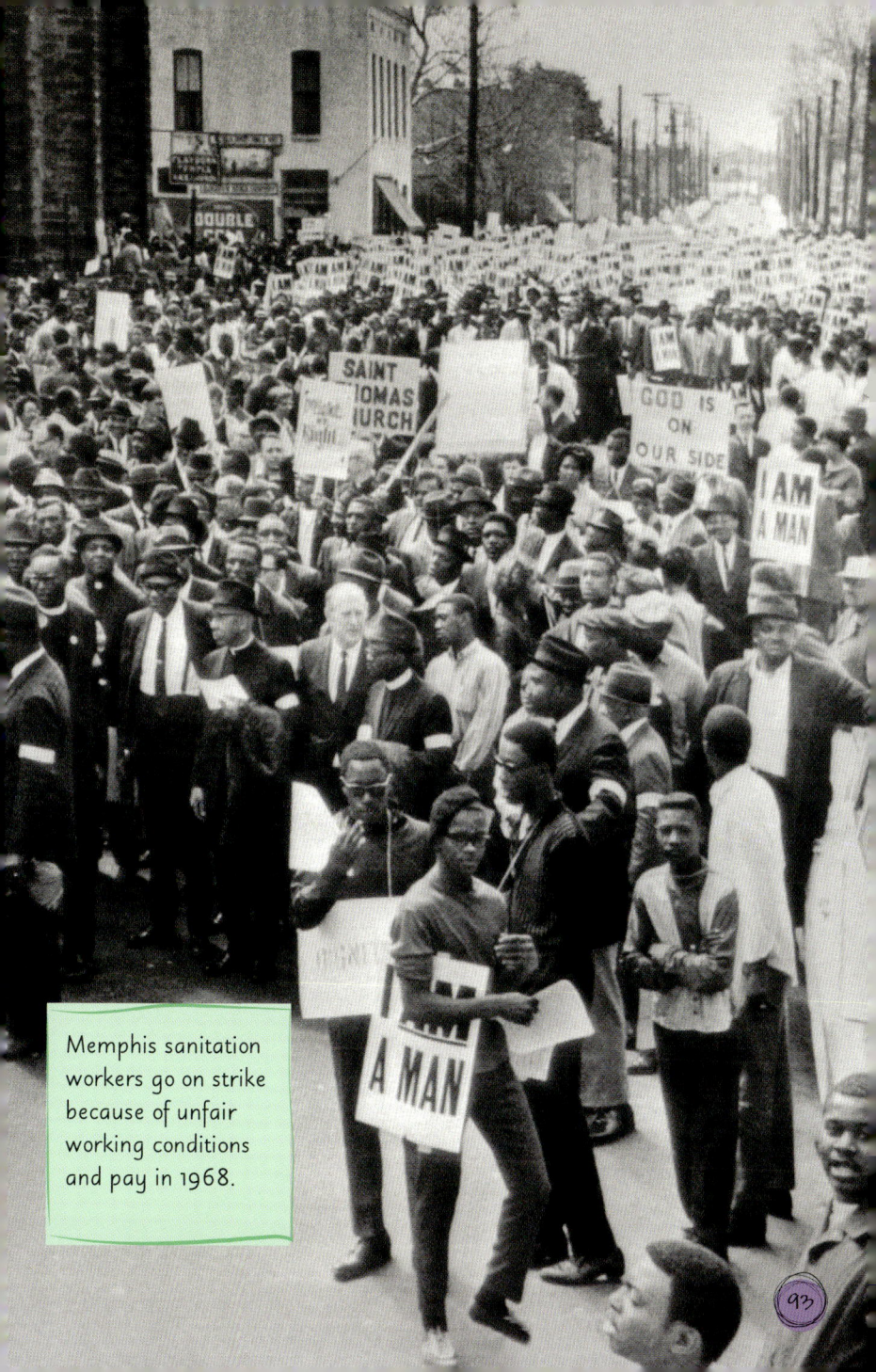

Memphis sanitation workers go on strike because of unfair working conditions and pay in 1968.

People were getting angry. Strike organizers worried that violence would break out. They asked Martin to come and speak. His staff urged him to stay focused on the Poor People's Campaign, but Martin couldn't say no to the black workers' call for help. He arrived in Memphis on 18 March 1968, and checked into the Lorraine Motel.

That night, Martin spoke at a rally in front of 17,000 people. He encouraged the strikers to stick together and keep going.

Today, the former Lorraine Motel in downtown Memphis is part of the National Civil Rights Museum.

He knew that they had to keep marching until they won their case.

Another protest march was scheduled, and Martin decided to lead it. More than 6,000 people were waiting for him to lead them to City Hall on 28 March. Martin sensed some tension in the crowd, but he had no idea that some young men were determined to get violent. He was waving to some fans when he heard the sound of breaking glass. Behind Martin, teenagers were smashing shop windows and stealing what they found inside. In front of Martin, police waited in full riot gear.

Martin had said he would never lead a violent march, and he immediately called it off. People did their best to get away from the scene while police fired tear gas and guns. By the time it was all over, 155 shops had been damaged, 60 people injured, and one teenager killed.

The violence made the national news. Martin was horrified. He couldn't stop thinking about the boy who had been killed. He knew he couldn't let the violent forces in the black community take over. He wanted to prove that a non-violent march was possible. This next march, he promised, would be better organized, and it would be peaceful.

On 3 April, Martin was back at the Lorraine Motel. He had received death threats. Someone had even said there was a bomb on his plane, but Martin persisted. That night, he spoke to a crowd of 2,000 people. Newspaper reporters and television cameras were there to record his speech.

Martin spoke without a script. He talked about the threats to his own life, but said that he wasn't afraid. He believed that he was doing

God's work. He knew there were difficult days ahead, but he believed they'd win in the end.

"And I may not get there with you," he said to the crowd. "But I want you to know tonight that we as a people will get to the Promised Land. So I'm happy tonight. I'm not worried about anything. I'm not fearing any man. Mine eyes have seen the glory of the coming of the Lord."

He finished his speech with the words of one of his favourite Negro spirituals – "Free at last! Free at last! Thank God Almighty we are free at last." Martin's speech was a huge success. It was televised all over the country.

He spent the next day, 4 April, organizing the march with his staff at the Lorraine Motel. They were getting ready to go out to dinner when Martin stepped out onto the balcony of his room, room 306. In an instant, he was struck by a bullet from a high-powered rifle. He was rushed to the hospital, but it was too late. Dr Martin Luther King Jr was dead.

"I want you to know tonight that we as a people will get to the Promised Land."

Martin Luther King Jr,
3 April 1968

Chapter 12

A lasting **legacy**

The loss of Martin was felt all over the world. His words and deeds have lived on, and his influence can still be felt today.

Coretta was on her way to the airport in Atlanta when she learned that Martin had been assassinated, or killed. She turned around and went home to comfort her children.

Soon the details of Martin's assassin were discovered. James Earl Ray was a racist and a criminal. He escaped from a Missouri prison in 1967 and spent the next year travelling around Canada, Mexico, and the United States. When he read about Martin's plans in Memphis, he had travelled there and waited. He shot

James Earl Ray

Martin from the window of a house near the Lorraine Motel, then fled the country. He was arrested in London, England, two months later. Ray confessed to the crime and was sentenced to 99 years in prison.

President Johnson announced that Sunday 7 April would be a national day of mourning. Flags were lowered to half mast around the country. Leaders from all over the world spoke out about Martin's life, and thousands of Americans marched, prayed, and sang songs in his honour. Most of the mourning was peaceful, but some black communities erupted in anger and violence.

SHOWING RESPECT

A flag flying at half mast, or half staff, is seen as a sign of respect and mourning in many countries around the world, including the United States.

Coretta knew Martin's work was far from finished. Days after his death, she and her children led protesters in a quiet, peaceful march in Memphis. A week later, the city recognized the sanitation workers' union and agreed to give the workers fair pay.

On 9 April, Martin was buried in Atlanta. The burial took place after a service at the Ebenezer Baptist Church, the same church that he had grown up in. His gravestone is inscribed with the words he loved: "Free at last. Free at last. Thank God Almighty I'm Free at last."

Coretta and their four children continued to carry his message and fight to make Martin's dream a reality, in the United States as well as in the rest of the world. So did many of Martin's followers.

On 9 April 1968, four days after Martin's death, Coretta leads a march for the sanitation workers' union in Memphis.

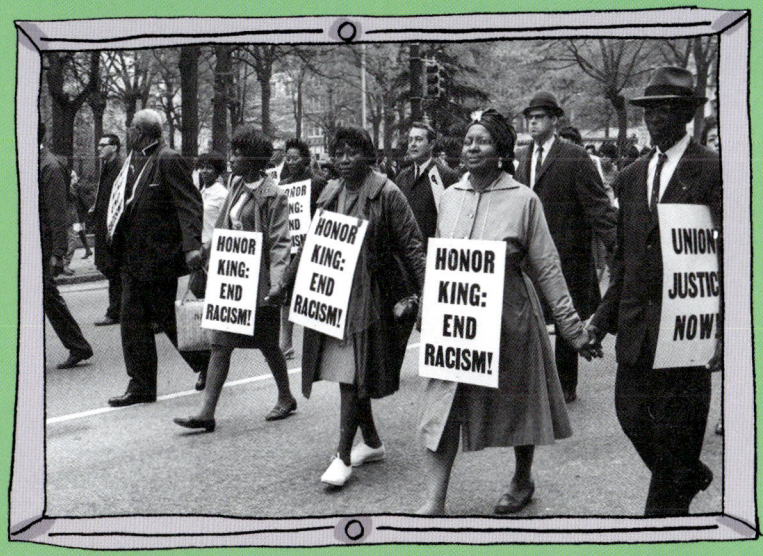

Protesters wearing signs that say "Honor King: End Racism!" march through the streets to show their support for equal rights.

Today, Martin and his teachings are studied by people all over the world. Parks, schools, and streets are named after him. In 1980, Martin's home on Auburn Avenue in Atlanta, the Ebenezer Baptist Church, and his burial site were named a National Historic Landmark. The nearby Martin Luther King Jr. Center for Nonviolent Social Change, which Coretta helped create in 1968, develops leaders who follow Martin's principles of non-violence as a way to make the world a better place.

In April 2016, the United States Treasury Department announced that Martin may one day join former president Abraham Lincoln on the five-dollar note, to honour his 1963 "I Have a Dream" speech at the Lincoln Memorial.

Coretta campaigned for 15 January, Martin's

What is a National Historic Landmark?   A place the government has recognized as extremely important to US history.

birthday, to be named a national holiday. It took many years and many meetings with politicians, but Coretta didn't give up. Finally, a bill sponsored by Senator Ted Kennedy, the younger brother of President Kennedy, was signed into law in 1983. The first Martin Luther King Jr. Day was celebrated in January 1986. People now celebrate the holiday in the United States on the third Monday in January.

A LIFE OF ACTIVISM

Coretta was an activist for equality and civil rights until her death in 2006. She is also remembered for promoting children's books. In 1969, the American Library Association began awarding the Coretta Scott King Book Awards to African-American writers and illustrators of the best books for children. Winners continue to be announced every January.

A display at the National Civil Rights Museum in Memphis honours the Montgomery bus boycott of 1955-1956.

Across the country, museums dedicated to preserving Martin's teachings and telling the story of the Civil Rights Movement continue to help keep his legacy alive. More than 300,000 visitors come to the National Civil Rights Museum in Memphis each year, and the Civil Rights Memorial in Montgomery honours the martyrs of the movement – including Martin.

What is a martyr? A person whose death inspires others to fight for their cause.

In 2016, the National Museum of African American History and Culture opened in Washington, D.C. The museum documents African-American life, art, history, and culture from the times of slavery to the present day. It often has special exhibits and celebrations in memory of Martin.

America has made some advances over the years, but the country continues to struggle

The National Museum of African American History and Culture had more than 700,000 visitors in its first year.

with some of the same problems Martin had tried to solve. Laws have been passed, and passionate people continue to fight for equality for all races. However, many African-Americans still live in ghettos and don't have the same educational opportunities as white people. Martin's dream may not yet have come true, but his words continue to inspire people everywhere who want to make the world a better place.

Martin's family tree

Martin Luther King Jr

1929–1968

Martin's first child, Yolanda, was an actor, producer, and public speaker.

Daughter

Yolanda Denise King

1955–2007

Timeline

1929 — Michael King Jr, who later became known as Martin Luther King Jr, is born on 15 January.

1944 — Martin begins attending Morehouse College in Atlanta at the age of 15.

1946 — Martin writes a letter to the *Atlanta Constitution* stating that African-Americans "are entitled to the basic rights and opportunities of American citizens."

1948 — Martin graduates from Morehouse and is appointed co-pastor at the Ebenezer Baptist Church in Atlanta.

Martin marries Coretta at the Scott family home near Marion, Alabama.

Activist Rosa Parks is arrested for refusing to give up her seat on a city bus to a white person. The Montgomery bus boycott begins.

1953　1954　1955　1956

Martin becomes the pastor of Dexter Avenue Baptist Church in Montgomery, Alabama.

The Montgomery bus boycott ends. Martin is one of the first passengers to board the newly integrated buses.

In January, southern black ministers meet in Atlanta to discuss how to fight against segregation. They create the Southern Christian Leadership Conference (SCLC) and name Martin its chairman.

The Civil Rights Act is signed. In the same year, Martin receives the Nobel Peace Prize.

In October, Martin is arrested after participating in a sit-in in Atlanta.

 1957

1960

1963

1964

In May, at the Lincoln Memorial in Washington, D.C., Martin delivers his "Give Us the Ballot" speech.

The March on Washington draws more than 200,000 people to the Lincoln Memorial. Martin delivers his "I Have a Dream" speech.

In March, Martin helps lead the five-day march from Selma to Montgomery in Alabama. In August, President Johnson signs the Voting Rights Act.

Martin is assassinated at the Lorraine Motel in Memphis, Tennessee.

1965

1967

1968

Martin announces his plan to organize the Poor People's Campaign in Washington, D.C.

Quiz

 In what year was Martin born?

 How old was Martin when he won first prize at a public-speaking contest?

 Who was the inspiring leader whose work made Martin believe in non-violent protest?

 To which southern city did Martin and Coretta move in September 1954?

 What do the letters in NAACP stand for?

 On the cover of which magazine did Martin appear in February 1957?

 On what two materials did Martin write his "Letter from Birmingham Jail"?

**Do you remember what you've read?
How many of these questions about
Martin's life can you answer?**

 What 1964 act made discrimination in public places and businesses illegal?

 What major award did Martin win in 1964?

 Who was the mayor of Chicago when Martin and his family moved there in 1966?

 What phrase was on the sanitation workers' signs during their strike in 1968?

 In which month are the Coretta Scott King Book Awards announced each year?

Answers on page 128

Who's who?

Anderson, Marian
(1897–1993) singer who performed at the March on Washington

Baez, Joan
(1941–) musician who performed at the March on Washington

Connor, Eugene "Bull"
(1897–1973) Commissioner of Public Safety in Birmingham, Alabama, who opposed the Civil Rights Movement

Daley, Richard J.
(1902–1976) mayor of Chicago, Illinois, from 1955 to 1976

Dylan, Bob
(1941–) musician who performed at the March on Washington

Eisenhower, Dwight D.
(1890–1969) president of the United States from 1953 to 1961

Evers, Medgar
(1925–1963) civil rights activist killed in 1963

Farris, Christine King
(1927–) Martin's older sister

Gandhi, Mohandas
(1869–1948) leader of the Indian independence movement

Johnson, Lyndon B.
(1908–1973) president of the United States from 1963 to 1969

Kennedy, John F.
(1917–1963) president of the United States from 1961 to 1963

Kennedy, Robert F.
(1925–1968) attorney general of the United States; President Kennedy's brother

Kennedy, Ted
(1932–2009) senator who sponsored a bill to make Martin's birthday a holiday

King, Alberta Williams (1904–1974) Martin's mother

King, Alfred Daniel (A.D.) Williams (1930–1969) Martin's younger brother

King, Bernice Albertine (1963–) Martin's younger daughter

King, Coretta Scott (1927–2006) Martin's wife

King, Dexter Scott (1961–) Martin's younger son

King, Martin Luther III (1957–) Martin's older son

King, Martin Luther Sr (1899–1984) Martin's father

King, Yolanda Denise (1955–2007) Martin's older daughter

Luther, Martin (1483–1546) religious thinker who began the Protestant Reformation

Malcolm X (1925–1965) leader, speaker, and activist who believed in using violence when necessary

Nixon, Richard M. (1913–1994) president of the United States from 1969 to 1974

Parks, Rosa (1913–2005) civil rights activist who played a vital role in the Montgomery bus boycott

Ray, James Earl (1928–1998) criminal who shot and killed Martin

Reeb, James (1927–1965) minister who was killed by the Ku Klux Klan in 1965

Thoreau, Henry David (1817–1862) writer who believed in civil disobedience

Glossary

act
law that the government has passed

activist
someone who takes action against something he or she feels is wrong

assassin
someone who kills a politician or religious leader

bail
money paid to free someone from police custody before he or she stands trial

bill
proposed new law

boycott
form of protest in which someone refuses to deal with a certain person or organization

civil disobedience
using peaceful methods when refusing to follow a law believed to be unfair

civil rights
rights to freedom and equality given by the US Constitution

communist
person who believes that the government should own everything and share its wealth and products between its citizens, or people

confrontation
meeting in which people challenge, or confront, one another

Congress
law-making branch of the US government

constitution
document listing the rights of a nation's citizens and how its government should work

FBI
Federal Bureau of Investigation – part of the US government that investigates crime

federal law
law that applies throughout the United States

ghetto
slum in which people of one religious group or race live

integration
bringing people of different races together to make sure they are treated equally

Jim Crow laws
unfair laws that discriminated against black people

Ku Klux Klan (KKK)
secret society violently opposed to the Civil Rights Movement and its beliefs

martyr
person whose death inspires others to fight for their cause

National Guard
military of a US state

Nobel Peace Prize
medal awarded each year in Oslo, Norway, to a person or group who has worked for world peace

philosopher
someone who thinks deeply about the nature of the world and life

policy
way that something is officially done

protest
to show that you disapprove of, or do not agree with, something

racism
belief that certain people are better than others because of their race, or hating a group of people because of their race

seamstress
woman whose job is sewing

segregation
keeping people of different races or religions separate from each other

seminary
school that trains clergy, such as priests

sharecropper
farmer who works a small plot of land owned by another farmer

sit-in
form of protest in which people sit in one place and refuse to leave

slum
poor, crowded, often dirty section of a city

solitary confinement
state of being kept isolated, or on your own, in prison

spiritual
type of religious song

state trooper
member of a US state's police force

strike
when workers refuse to work in order to convince or force their employer to meet their demands

Supreme Court
highest court in the United States

tear gas
chemical that temporarily blinds people by stinging their eyes and producing tears; sometimes used by police to control crowds

Index

16th Street Church
(Birmingham) 61, 70

Aa
Albany, Georgia 55–56
arrests 50, 51, 56, 59–60, 76
assassination 98, 100
Atlanta, Georgia 8, 9, 32, 48, 51, 79, 102

Bb
Birmingham, Alabama 54, 58–62, 70–71
Bloody Sunday 79
bomb attacks 40–41, 54, 58, 62, 70, 96
Boston, Massachusetts 28, 30–32
boycotts 38–45, 106
Brown v. Board of Education 47
bus boycott, Montgomery 38–45, 106

Cc
Chicago 85, 86, 87–88
Children's Crusade 61–62
cinemas 17, 49, 53
civil disobedience 23
Civil Rights Act 72, 73

civil rights bill 52, 62, 65, 72
Civil Rights Movement 59, 68, 71, 74, 84, 89
  anthem 56, 66
  birth of 44
  martyrs 106
  spread of 46–63
Civil War 35, 40
Clark, Jim 75, 76
Confederate states 35
confrontation 59
Congress 62, 65, 72, 90
Connor, Eugene "Bull" 58, 61
Coretta Scott King Book Awards 105
Crozer Theological Seminary 24–29

Dd
Daley, Richard J. 88
death threats 96
Dexter Avenue Baptist Church (Montgomery) 34

Ee
Ebenezer Baptist Church 8, 10, 24, 25, 32, 48, 70, 102, 104
Eckford, Elizabeth 47

education 20, 21, 22–29, 30
Eisenhower, Dwight D. 47
Evers, Medgar 64

Ff
family background 8–12
FBI 90
five-dollar notes 104
flags, at half mast 101
Freedom Riders 54–55, 58
Freedom Summer 75
funeral 102

Gg
Gandhi, Mohandas 26–27, 48
Georgia State Prison 51
graduation 28–29
grave 102, 104
Greenboro, North Carolina 48–49

Ii
"I Have a Dream" 68, 104
India 27, 48
integration 46, 47–49, 78

Jj
Jackson, Mississippi 64
Jim Crow laws 13–14, 17, 20, 34–35, 65
Johnson, Lyndon B. 71, 72, 73, 81, 88, 90, 101

Kk
Kennedy, John F. 51, 52, 62, 63, 71, 72, 90
Kennedy, Robert F. 52, 55, 66
Kennedy, Ted 105
King, Alberta 10, 15, 17, 19
King, Alfred Daniel (A. D.) 11–12, 15, 16–17
King, Bernice 58
King, Christine 11, 15, 29
King, Coretta Scott 28, 31–35, 36–37, 38, 40, 46–47, 51, 58, 86, 100, 102, 103, 104, 105
King, Dexter 52, 58
King, Martin Sr 8–11, 15, 19–20, 24, 28, 32, 48
King, Martin Luther III 47, 58
King, Yolanda 37, 40, 47, 58
Ku Klux Klan (KKK) 40, 70, 75, 81

Ll
legacy 100–108
"Letter from Birmingham Jail" 60
Lincoln, Abraham 104
Little Rock (Arkansas) 47
Lorraine Motel (Memphis) 94, 96, 98, 101, 106
Luther, Martin 12

Mm

Malcolm X 78
marriage 31–33
Martin Luther King Jr Day 105
Martin Luther King Jr. Center for Nonviolent Social Change 104
Memphis, Tennessee 92–99, 100–101, 103, 106
Montgomery, Alabama 34–35, 36–45, 48, 54, 78, 81, 83
Montgomery Improvement Association 39, 43
Morehouse College (Atlanta) 10, 16, 22–23, 29

Nn

name-calling 17, 35
Nashville, Tennessee 53
National Association for the Advancement of Colored People (NAACP) 36, 38, 64
National Civil Rights Museum (Memphis) 106
National Guard 55
National Historic Landmarks 70, 104
National Museum of African American History and Culture (Washington) 107
New York City 85, 86
Nixon, Richard M. 51
Nobel Peace Prize 74
non-violent protest 23, 26, 27, 30, 40, 48, 55, 59, 60, 71, 78, 83, 88, 89, 90, 96, 104

Oo

Obama, Barack 71

Pp

Parks, Rosa 36–38, 45, 106
pay, African-Americans 11
Poor People's Campaign 90, 94
poverty 72, 84–91, 108
presidential election 51
Project C 59, 62
protest marches 56, 59, 61, 62, 65–69, 76–77, 78–80, 90, 92, 95, 96, 102–103
public-speaking contest 20

Qq

quotes 18, 20, 42, 57, 90, 97, 99

Rr

racism 16–20, 27, 35, 90, 103
Ray, James Earl 100–101
Reagan, Ronald 105
rented accommodation 30, 32, 86–88
riots 56, 62, 71, 85, 95

Ss

sanitation workers' union (Memphis) 92–94, 103
schools, integration 47–49
schools, segregation 9–10, 72
segregation 10–11, 13–14, 20–21, 26, 27, 44, 47, 48–53, 54, 72, 86, 88
Selma, Alabama 75–83
Selma to Montgomery walk 78–81
sermons 24, 25, 34, 70
sit-ins 49, 52, 53, 56
slavery 23
slums 84, 86
Southern Christian Leadership Conference (SCLC) 46, 58–59, 60, 65
speeches 20, 46, 67–69, 74, 94, 96–99, 104
stand-in-line protests 53
stores 11, 48–53, 59
strikes 92–94

Student Nonviolent Coordination Committee (SNCC) 49, 51, 55, 75
student protests 47, 48–49, 52, 54, 75

Tt

Thoreau, Henry David 23, 26
transport 11, 13, 20, 21, 35, 37, 44, 45

Uu

US Supreme Court 43–44, 45, 47

Vv

Vietnam War 88–90
vote, registering to 11, 14, 36, 72, 75, 76, 78–81, 84
Voting Rights Act 81, 85

Ww

Wallace, George 78
Washington, D.C. 62, 65–69, 90, 107
Where Do We Go From Here: Chaos or Community? 90, 91
white supremacists 64
Williams, A. D. 8
Woolworth store 48–49, 52

Acknowledgements

DK would like to thank: Romi Chakraborty and Pallavi Narain for design support; Lindsay Walter-Greaney for proofreading; Helen Peters for the index; Jolyon Goddard for additional editorial work; and Victoria Pyke for Anglicization.

The publisher would like to thank the following for their kind permission to reproduce their photographs:

(Key: a-above; b-below/bottom; c-centre; f-far; l-left; r-right; t-top)

7 Library of Congress, Washington, D.C.: LC-USZ62-116775 (ca). 9 Library of Congress, Washington, D.C.: LC-DIG-highsm-47144 (cra). 12 Alamy Stock Photo: Quagga Media (clb). 13 Getty Images: William Lovelace / Stringer. 15 Library of Congress, Washington, D.C.: LC-USZ62-124909 (ca). Mary Evans Picture Library: Everett Collection (cb). 23 Alamy Stock Photo: Historical image collection by Bildagentur-online 2. 25 Getty Images: Donald Uhrbrock / The LIFE Picture Collection. 27 Getty Images: ullstein bild Dtl.. 29 Morehouse College. 31 Alamy Stock Photo: Photo 12 (cra). 33 Bridgeman Images. 37 Getty Images: Michael Ochs Archives / Stringer (cra). 38 Getty Images: Photo 12 (cla). 45 Getty Images: Don Cravens / The LIFE Picture Collection (cla, cra, cb). 49 Rex by Shutterstock: Granger. 50 Getty Images: Donald Uhrbrock / The LIFE Picture Collection. 51 Getty Images: Alfred Eisenstaedt / Pix Inc. / The LIFE Picture Collection. 53 Getty Images: Bettmann (cb); Howard Sochurek / The LIFE Picture Collection (ca). 55 Getty Images: Bettmann. 58 Alamy Stock Photo: Walter Oleksy. 61 Alamy Stock Photo: Everett Collection Historical. 64 Getty Images: Hulton Archive. 69 Getty Images: Bettmann. 70 Alamy Stock Photo: Ian Dagnall. 72 Library of Congress, Washington, D.C.: LC-USZ62-13036 (cra). 73 Getty Images: Photo 12. 75 Photo courtesy of Global Ministries of The United Methodist Church: Ken Thompson. 77 Alamy Stock Photo: Everett Collection Historical (ca). Getty Images: Bettmann (cb). 78 Library of Congress, Washington, D.C.: LC-USZ62-119478. 79 Getty Images: Steve Schapiro / Corbis Premium Historical. 82–83 Getty Images: Bettmann. 87 Getty Images: Bettmann. 88 Library of Congress, Washington, D.C.: LC-U9- 33303-23. 89 Getty Images: Hulton Archive / Blank Archives. 93 Getty Images: Bettmann. 94 Dreamstime.com: F11photo. 100 Getty Images: Bettmann. 101 123RF.com: Susan Montgomery. 103 Getty Images: Bettmann (ca); Robert Abbott Sengstacke (cb). 106 Dreamstime.com: Calvin L. Leake. 107 Dreamstime.com: Luiz Gustavo Freitas Rossi. 109 Getty Images: Flip Schulke Archives / Corbis Premium Historical. 110 Library of Congress, Washington, D.C.: LC-USZ62-116775 (cl)

Cover images: *Front and Spine*: Bridgeman Images: Photo © AGIP; Reprinted by arrangement with the Heirs to the Estate of Martin Luther King Jr, c/o Writers House as agent for the proprietor New York, NY: © 1966 Dr Martin Luther King Jr. © copyright renewed 1994 Coretta Scott King

All other images © Dorling Kindersley
For further information see: www.dkimages.com

ANSWERS TO THE QUIZ ON PAGES 116–117

1. 1929; 2. 14 years old; 3. Mohandas Gandhi, or Mahatma Gandhi; 4. Montgomery, Alabama; 5. The National Association for the Advancement of Colored People; 6. *Time* magazine; 7. newspaper and toilet paper; 8. Civil Rights Act; 9. Nobel Peace Prize; 10. Richard J. Daley; 11. "I AM A MAN"; 12. January